Alexandra Griesing

Harriet Beecher Stowe´s
Uncle Tom´s Cabin

The Creation and influence
of a masterpiece

Anchor Compact

Griesing, Alexandra: Harriet Beecher Stowe´s Uncle Tom´s Cabin: The Creation and influence of a masterpiece. Hamburg, Diplomica Verlag GmbH 2012
Original title of the thesis: The slave "who caused that great war" – Uncle Tom´s Cabin in print and on stage

ISBN: 978-3-95489-034-7
Print: Anchor Academic Publishing, an Imprint of Diplomica® Verlag GmbH, Hamburg, 2012
Additionally: Georg-August-Universität Göttingen, Göttingen, Deutschland, Bachelorarbeit, May 2009

Bibliographical Information of the German National Library:
The German National Library lists this publication in the German National Bibliography. Detailed bibliographic data can be found at: http://dnb.d-nb.de

The digital publication (eBook) of this work with the ISBN 978-3-95489-534-2 can be purchased on the general market or directly from the publisher.

© Anchor Academic Publishing, ein Imprint der Diplomica® Verlag GmbH
http://www.diplom.de, Hamburg 2012
Printed in Germany

Table of Contents

0. Introduction

"So you´re the little woman who wrote the book that started this great war"
(Raabe 216)! With these words Abraham Lincoln is said to have greeted
Harriet Beecher Stowe when she visited the white House in 1863. Without
doubt, *Uncle Tom´s Cabin*, Stowe´s first antislavery novel, was one of the
most controversial books when it was published in 1851/52. Although it
certainly can´t be seen as the true reason for the Civil War that started in
1861, it nevertheless put the debate on slavery more strongly in the center of
public attention.

This paper deals with this highly controversial book. First, the context of
the writing as well as the publishing of *Uncle Tom´s Cabin* will be presented,
and its sources will be outlined. For a better understanding of the
circumstances, some biographical pieces of information about the author will
be given beforehand. The next section will focus on the several stage
adaptations of *Uncle Tom´s Cabin*, the one by George L. Aiken will already
be treated in more detail. The mixed reactions towards Stowe´s novel in
general will be delineated, too. After giving a summary of the content of
Uncle Tom´s Cabin to establish the basis for a further analysis, the main part
of this paper will deal with the comparison of the novel with Aiken´s most -as
far as the structure, the characters and the themes are concerned. This paper
will try to show that Aiken´s version of *Uncle Tom´s Cabin* comes very close
to Stowe´s novel, but that he incorporated his own ideas as well to partly
produce other effects, too.

1. Harriet Beecher Stowe

Harriet Beecher Stowe was born in Litchfield, Connecticut, on June 14, 1811.
Her father Lyman Beecher, who was an influential minister of the
Congregational Church and a rigorous Calvinist, was head of the household
since Stowe´s mother had died early in 1816. Stowe, the seventh of nine
children, was shaped by daily religious instructions and family worship.
Religion decidedly played a central role in the life of her family. "Because of
her father´s focus on his sons´ mental and intellectual preparation as future
ministers, Harriet often felt neglected" (Wurst 2449). Her sister Catherine
became a strong influence in her life. When she was twelve years old, Stowe

was put under the direction of her disciplinary sister at the Hartford Female Seminary, who "consecrated herself to the cause of female education" (Adams 22).

In 1832, her family reunited and moved to Cincinnatti, Ohio (Adams 2123). Very soon she met Calvin E. Stowe, a biblical scholar, whom she married in 1836 (Wurst 2449). From then on she was busy caring for her growing family. The marriage produced seven children. During that time of her life, Stowe was still disappointed and unhappy. Not only was she controlled by her husband and her conduct regulated by him, but she had to live in poverty and was strongly bound to her household tasks. She felt constrained. What bothered her the most were her money problems. To help support the family financially, she dedicated herself to writing. Later in her life, Stowe would say that she primarily "wrote for money" (Adams 25). Her husband supported her literary career, but her bad physical condition sometimes kept her from writing.

Altogether, Stowe spent about eighteen years in Cincinnatti. Although it was a period of poverty and distress, it was nevertheless a period rich in observation and experience (Anthony 117). "It was there that she first visited a plantation in neighboring Kentucky and was introduced directly to issues of slavery, because in Cincinnatti, there were many freed and fugitive slaves" (Wurst 2449). On the plantation, Stowe saw the life of the slaves in their cabins. To the impressions she gained there those of her brother, who had been to New Orleans and ascended the Red River, were added (Anthony 117). In Cincinnatti she also became familiar with the abolitionist movement and the "underground railroad." Although these experiences had a deep impact on her, it took her several years to digest these things and write about them (Ellis 1247). "It was not until her return to New England in 1850 during the discussion over the Fugitive Slave Law, that her antislavery feeling became intense" (Anthony 117).

Before she left Cincinnatti for her home New England, she suffered a stroke of fate. In 1849 her oneyearold son Samuel Charles died of cholera. "It was at his dying bed and at his grave," Stowe wrote of Charley in a letter, "that I learned what a poor slave mother may feel when her child is torn away from her" (Stowe (2007) 21). One year later she started writing *Uncle Tom's Cabin* at Brunswick. The novel was published in 1851/52, followed by *A Key* to *"Uncle Tom's Cabin"* in 1853. Three years later she wrote *Dred: A Tale of Great Dismal Swamp*, another antislavery novel, published in 1856. The pen forever remained her most powerful antislavery weapon (Hedrick 906/07). Legend has it, that when Stowe came to the White House in 1862, president Abraham Lincoln greeted her as "'the little lady who wrote the book that made this big war!'" It is more than doubtful that the book caused the Civil War, but, nevertheless, the legend shows that Stowe had become a famous public figure, and that *Uncle Tom's Cabin* exercised a great influence on public opinion (Adams 8/9).

After the Civil War, Stowe was again busy writing books, mainly New England and society novels. She poured forth a steady stream of fiction publishing on the average almost a book a year until she ended her literary career in 1878 (Anthony 119). Throughout her career she used literature to have a political voice, and shape public opinion. "She urged the nation to civil disobedience, challenged religious orthodoxy, and dared to discuss incest – all in the name of motherhood, Christianity, and democracy" (Hedrick 908). Never did she have the success she had with *Uncle Tom's Cabin* again. Her eventual conviction that her bestselling novel was written by God has been much ridiculed (Wagenknecht 162). However, one has to keep in mind that in her final years, her mind at times wandered. She died on July 1, 1896 in Litchfield, Connecticut (Wurst 2450).

2. The Writing and Publishing of *Uncle Tom's Cabin*

When Stowe began writing her famous novel she was about forty years old and in poor shape. She had been living in poverty with her family for a long time, was sick and exhausted from trying to fulfil her roles as a good wife, mother, and housewife. She had been subservient for all her life, felt miserable, and even compared her situation to that of a slave (Adams 44). In her own words, *Uncle Tom's Cabin* was "her declaration of independence, … her emancipation proclamation" (Adams 27). "Into *Uncle Tom's Cabin* … Mrs. Stowe was able to pour her whole life … ." Before the book's success, she was harassed by debt and unknown; after it, she was wealthy and famous (Adams 45/46). And *Uncle Tom's Cabin* made her more than just famous – it made her immortal.

Before she wrote *Uncle Tom's Cabin*, Stowe had already published stories in which she treated the issue of slavery, e.g. "The Freeman's Dream: A Parable". Nevertheless, the effectiveness of these works was rather weak. "Compared with this crude effort, *Uncle Tom's Cabin* would be a masterpiece of persuasion" (Gossett 89). After the passage of the Fugitive Slave Law, which was part of the Compromise of 1850, Stowe at last set out to write an antislavery novel. It is said that her sisterinlaw, Mrs Edward Beecher, exerted the final influence on Stowe when writing a letter to her toward the end of 1850. She is quoted as saying, "'Now, Hattie, if I could just use the pen as you can, I would write something that would make this whole nation feel what an accursed thing slavery is'" (Anthony 117). Reading the passage aloud to her family, Stowe "rose from her chair, crushed the letter in her hand, and … said, 'I will write something. I will if I live'" (Gossett 90). And so she did, although it wasn't easy for her. Still she had to care for her children and the house in Brunswick, Maine, where she had been living since the spring of 1850. And she was all alone, her husband Calvin being away in Cincinnatti. To him she wrote that she was thinking of writing a sketch for the *National Era* (Gossett 8791). It wasn't long afterward that Stowe imagined the character of Uncle Tom. There are different stories about how she imagined his death scene. Once she said that during a communion service in Brunswick, "she had what she could only describe as a 'vision' of the scene which illustrated the worst possible evil of slavery – death by torture" (Gossett 91). Another time she said that the scene arose before her when she was lying down to rest after lunch one day. "In the introduction to the 1879 edition of *Uncle Tom's Cabin*, Stowe told how she had written the whipping scene of Uncle Tom before anything else in the novel … " (Gossett 92).

As she had planned it, *Uncle Tom's Cabin* first appeared as a serial in the antislavery journal *National Era*. At the beginning she had no intention of writing a novel. To Gamaliel Bailey, the publisher of the newspaper, she wrote that she thought of her story extending through four issues of the weekly journal. In the same letter she explained that it would be a series of sketches about the "patriarchal institution," and that the incidents described would have occurred in the sphere of her observation or her personal knowledge. Stowe was paid $300 for the story and received additional $100, as her story in the end didn't extend through four, but through more than thirty issues of the *National Era* (Gossett 97). The journal printed Stowe's story from June 5, 1851, to April 1, 1852 (Wurst 2451). In 1852 *Uncle Tom's Cabin* was published in book form by J. P. Jewett (Hedrick 907). There were two volumes, "with a woodcut of a negro cabin as the frontispiece" (Anthony 117). Within the first week of its publication, ten thousand copies were sold. "The first edition, consisting of 5,000 copies, was bought out in just two days … " (Hill 53). Within a year, the story sold more than threehundred thousand copies solely in the United States. The sales in Europe were not less phenomenal. In one year, forty different editions were published in Great Britain and its colonies; overall, 1.5 million copies were sold. The story was translated into dozens of languages and dialects. In Germany, a total of seventyfive editions were printed. Even in Italy, Stowe had great success with her first novel, although it was banned by the Catholic Church (Hill 53). Not only was *Uncle Tom's Cabin* translated into many languages, and were hundreds of editions printed all over the world, but it was immediately put on stage, and "embodied in popular culture in the form of songs, toys, and figurines" (Hedrick 907).

3. Sources of Uncle Tom's Cabin

People have agreed on Theodore Weld's *American Slavery As It Is* (1839) being a major source for Stowe's antislavery novel. In the preface to the 1878 edition of her book she explicitly acknowledges the use of Weld's wellknown propaganda book for abolition (Adams 57). *American Slavery As It Is* was "a collection of excerpts from legal documents, advertisements, and statements from slaveholders" (Wurst 2450).

Stowe owed much to Weld, but she made use of other sources as well. *Uncle Tom's Cabin* shares similarities with other abolitionist novels, e.g. with Richard Hildreth's *The Slave: or Memoirs of Archy Moore* (1836). The character of Archy reminds one of George Harris, and the cruel overseer of the novel is a Northerner – just like Legree. Cassy suggests an appropriate comparison with Eliza, and there is even a character similar to Uncle Tom, namely the slave Thomas. Both Uncle Tom and Thomas are of unmixed African blood, gentle, and pious Christians. Although several common features can be recognized, Stowe never admitted acquaintance with Hildreth's antislavery novel (Adams 57; Gossett 154).

The autobiography of Josiah Henson[1] has also been identified as an authentic source for parts of *Uncle Tom's Cabin*. His character can well be compared with that of Uncle Tom. Henson himself claims to have provided Stowe with the originals of George Harris, Eliza, Topsy, Legree, St. Clare and Eva in the persons of friends and particular acquaintances. In fact, Stowe knew Henson's autobiography very well (Adams 56). Still, opinion is deeply divided on this issue. Some people think that Stowe simply copied certain things from other books and built on the reports of others, while other people are sure that she derived her materials mainly from personal experience and observation. It is said that when Stowe visited a plantation in Kentucky in 1833, she observed everything and thereby got all she needed for the depiction of the Shelby plantation (Wagenknecht 157). As far as the characters are concerned, among other things, it is assumed that the human original of Topsy was a black girl named Celeste, whom the Beechers came to know in Cincinnati. The human original of Eliza is supposed to have been a fugitive, whom Stowe's father had helped (Adams 56). Nevertheless, several originals have been suggested for the different characters. It is not clear which source is the right one.

Other great writers of that time seem to have influenced Stowe, too. The character of Eva shows some similarities with Charles Dickens' Nell. Topsy suggests comparison with Pearl of Nathaniel Hawthorne's masterpiece *The Scarlet Letter*. "Neither Hawthorne nor Stowe was convinced that children are inherently innocent" (Gossett 132/33).

Some themes of *Uncle Tom's Cabin* have their source from very personal events in the life of Stowe. "In her depiction of Eva's death, she may owe something to family accounts of her own mother's death. Lyman Beecher had seen the moment of Roxana's dying as her grand entrance into heaven" (Gossett 143).

Stowe as a professional writer used all the sources she could use to write *Uncle Tom's Cabin*. The most important sources were probably her own experience and observations. Only because of that was she able to write her novel with such a passion like she did.

---

1   An escaped slave who escaped to Ontario, Canada in 1830.

4. Adaptations of the Novel

"Despite the popularity of Stowe´s novel, most Americans probably got their Uncle Tom experience from one of the myriad performances on stage" (Richards 371). Stowe´s novel was complex. The melodramatic scenes and the vivid characters in *Uncle Tom´s Cabin* provided great material for dramatic productions (Toll 90). Therefore, it is not surprising that at about the same time, when the novel was published in book form, there were several adaptations of *Uncle Tom´s Cabin* with which Stowe had no connection – never did a playwright seek for her permission to bring a play based on the content of her famous novel on the stage – and from which she gained no profit. "Some scripts followed a simple theme and were almost sketches; other versions lasted as long as five hours and included some fifty scenes" (Meserve 113). Be that as it may, these adaptations misrepresented her novel to such a degree "that it still controls some people´s reactions to the author" (Adams 7). Weak copyright laws in the United States provided for the novel´s title, characters, and plot devices being taken and used in different ways. All across the nation theaters put on socalled "Tom shows." Most of the productions didn´t have anything in common with the original novel except the title or the names of the characters e.g. (Gardner 165). "By 1900 there were twelve different playscripts in print and probably many more pirated and adapted versions were staged but never published" (Hill 53). As a matter of fact, some of the versions were well performed into the 20th century. About fifty troups toured the United States in 1879, and there were still twelve companies which performed *Uncle Tom´s* Cabin in 1927 (Bordman 685). Even in England, people were scrambling to get *Uncle Tom´s* Cabin on the stage. Eight versions of the play are solely recorded in London during 1852. No other play can show a comparable variety in the stage versions. Not without good reason does the play deserve the title "The World´s Greatest Hit" (Meserve 108, 11213). Those who don´t completely agree with that must at least acknowledge that "*Uncle Tom´s* Cabin was one of the most important documents in American dramatic history." Every major American actor or actress had played one of the characters from the famous novel (Miller 22).

In the United States, Charles Western Taylor brought the first important version to the stage. His play had its premiere at New York´s National Theatre in August 1852. It was the first abolitionist document to reach the stage, and, besides, there was a second novelty: for the first time, blacks appeared as leading characters in a drama (Miller 22). Before, the stage Negro had the character of a clownish servant and was spoofed (Meserve 73). Clifton Tayleure put a popular version on stage in Detroit in October 1852. H. J. Conway´s version, which was the most famous proSouthern version of *Uncle Tom´s Cabin,* ran in Boston for two hundred nights, and was eventually staged by the famous showman P. T. Barnum at his multimedia museum in New York in November 1853. Barnum claimed that Conway´s version would give a "'true picture of negro life in the South'" by showing the cruelties of the institution of slavery without unjustly elevating blacks above the white race in morals or intellect. The production had a happy ending with Uncle Tom being finally rescued from cruel Legree´s plantation (Richards 369; Toll 91). A few years later there were four rival productions solely in New York, with or without a happy ending. Many of these productions of the drama "carried a chorus of authentic blacks to sing and dance plantation and jubilee songs and to perform socalled Negro specialities" (Hill 56).

The characters in the plays, whether black or white, became stereotypes. These stereotypes ingrained themselves in the consciousness of the people, and one mustn´t forget that the representation of blacks on stage had profound social and cultural impacts and effects (Bryer 6). A range of serious actors resented this stereotyping of blacks and planned to establish their own theater companies. Usually, that is to say, it was the case that white actors played the roles of the Negro characters. They used dark makeup and spoke in the Negro dialect. The superiority of the white race was often more emphasized when the actors playing Eliza and George Harris, the two mulattoes of the story, used nearly no makeup at all. In the majority of cases, only Topsy, the minor Negro characters, and sometimes Uncle Tom were played as identifiable Negroes with actors being painted black (Hill 56/57). There had already been Negro parts in one or two plays, and blackface singers, in fact, were known at the beginning of the 19th century, but in the course of this century, the conventional stereotype was eventually introduced (Miller 21). "Until the end of the 19th century, the stage Negro continued his stereotype as part minstrel and part noble savage. And he was in nearly all cases played by white actors in blackface" (Miller 23). Sam Lucas would be the first African American to play the role of Uncle Tom, more than twenty years after the role was performed for the first time (Hill 56).

Although there were innumerable dramatizations, in the end, it was only one "which made history –" (Wagenknecht 17) the one by George Aiken from 1852. "Of all the stage versions, Aiken's comes closest to matching the novel" (Richards 371).

4.1. George Aiken's Version of *Uncle Tom's Cabin*

The immense success of his dramatization of *Uncle Tom's Cabin* – the third adaptation of the narrative (Hill 53) must have been a big surprise. "Aiken's version was said to be the first play offered on Broadway as an entire evening, without an afterpiece or any other entertainment" (Bordman 685). It was "the only one of the many 19th century dramatizations of *Uncle Tom's Cabin* that was regularly published" (Railton). William Lloyd Garrison, the editor of the antislavery newspaper *Liberator*, who had criticized Stowe's novel blisteringly, mainly for being in favor of colonization, praised his stage version to the skies (Toll 90).

Aiken, born in Boston on December 19, 1830, had always been interested in acting and the theater, in which he was influenced by his cousin Caroline Fox, who was an actress, but he couldn't start acting himself before 1849. From then on, he had a few minor roles with smaller companies in Rhode Island (Gardner 166). He probably would have gone on like that, had not the husband of his cousin Caroline, George C. Howard, the theater manager of the Troy Museum in New York, asked him to write a version of *Uncle Tom's Cabin*, in which his talented fouryearold daughter was supposed to play the role of Eva, and come to be known. "For a bonus of $40 and a gold watch, Aiken worked for a week to shape the play around the character of little Eva" (Nathans 14). This original version of the novel covered up to Eva's death. The play was put on stage for the first time at the Troy Museum in September of 1852, with Cordelia Howard starring Eva. Aiken himself played the role of both George Harris and George Shelby, and his cousin Caroline as well as her husband were involved in the play, too. Caroline played the role of Topsy while her husband scintillated as St. Clare (Gardner 166).

Later, Aiken would write a sixact version that moved to the end of the novel. His play was such a success that people asked Aiken to mount a sequel, which showed the rest of Stowe's original story. On the whole there were "five different major productions of Aiken's version of *Uncle Tom's Cabin* between 1852 and 1858" (Railton). *The Death of Uncle Tom; or, The Religion of the Lowly*, as it was called, had its first performance in November of 1852, and was combined with his original version of the play to create a complete version of the international bestseller (Nathans 14). After the play had run for more than a hundred nights, Aiken and his crew were engaged by the National Theatre in New York. A. H. Purdy, who had also staged Taylor´s version, had asked him to bring his play to a bigger stage in New York. Purdy´s production of Aiken´s version was performed 325 times. The play ran from July 18, 1853, to May 13, 1854 (Richards 371). Although Aiken had by that time other successes in the theater and even took over as the manager of the theater in Troy in 1861, he never "saw the kind of success he had with *Uncle Tom´s Cabin* again" (Gardner 167).

While adaptations of the novel before the Civil War, including Aiken´s version, more or less shared an antislavery message, after the war, the different productions of the play lost their antislavery emphasis. Early American drama mirrored the social and political movements of its day (Meserve 120). ProSouthern versions of the play actually "proved more in touch with the general public´s tastes" (Toll 92). This unavoidably had the effect that its antislavery theme was weakened. As a result of that, black characters became increasingly stereotyped. The productions of the play became comic treatments of blacks and had mainly sentimental and melodramatic devices. Simon Legree got meaner and meaner, and by 1879, dogs were integrated in the play which pursued Eliza (Meserve 113). "Uncle Tom himself very often didn´t become a man of dignity, as might be expected, but a mere figure of pathos, and the character of Topsy and the minor Negroes was so extremely exaggerated that one couldn´t easily distinguish them from the blacks of the popular minstrel shows" (Gossett 367). Minstrels had very soon incorporated *Uncle Tom´s Cabin* in their shows. Parodies such as "Uncle Tom and His Cabin" or "Uncle Dad´s Cabin" were performed successfully. The portrait of a dumb, dancing Negro was common in minstrel playlets. And they spared noone, not even Uncle Tom, a man of morality, spirituality, and humanity like no other. In the blackface minstrelsy, Uncle Tom was given dancing scenes and silly dialogue, and *Uncle Tom´s Cabin* was retitled "Happy Uncle Tom" (Toll 9294). "On stage, minstrelsy repeatedly acted out images which illustrated that there was no need to fight a war over slavery, no need to accept Negroes as equals in the North … " (Toll 97). John E. Owens would later adapt and soften Aiken's version of the drama to accommodate the audience. He himself would play the role of Uncle Tom as a lowcomedy type (Toll 92).

"Aiken's work as a playwright demonstrates two prevailing influences on American popular culture in the years before the Civil War: the minstrel show and melodrama" (Nathans 14). As the producer of a play for the theaters, he had another audience in mind, to whose expectations he had to come up to, than Stowe with her novel. To please that part of his audience familiarized with minstrel routines and Jim Crow dances, Aiken overstated Topsy in a way that he gave her excessive dancing and comic scenes, and, for that purpose, modified her dialogues (Nathans 15). Thomas Dartmouth "Jim Crow" Rice invented the Negro minstrel show in 1828. Even though actors had already impersonated Negroes on stage for more than thirty years, Rice was seen as the "Father of American Minstrelsy," as he had performed a single blackface act. Jokes and music acts steadily belonged to a blackface minstrelsy. Usually, the banjo and the tambourine were played. While in the early stages, minstrel companies consisted of only a few people, by the end of the 19th century such companies included a hundred people or even more. The minstrel evolved into a real spectacle show. "It is generally agreed that the minstrel show is America's original contribution to world theater … ." The minstrelsies and the "Tom shows" had one particular thing in common: they aroused attention and created excitement in a way that they "reached out to the average man and made him laugh and cry" (Meserve 74, 10911).

Melodramatic influence is exerted on the treatment of the characters Uncle Tom, Eliza, and Eva, all of whom play the roles of the typical hero or heroine of melodrama by demonstrating virtue and altruism (Nathans 15). "Melodrama may be recognized by its excess of pathos and the dichotomy of good and bad. Character and plot are secondary to dramatic situations which combine theatrical spectacle, scenographic realism and sensational action" (Herget 21). Usually, a melodrama ends with a happy ending, but tragedies "that use much of the same technique" are also seen as melodramatic. That's the case with *Uncle Tom's Cabin*. The object of a melodrama is "to keep the audience thrilled by the arousal of strong feelings of pity, horror, or joy"

(Tennyson 317). In a melodrama, music plays a very important role. This can be seen in Aiken's play as well, in which many singing and dancing scenes with music are included. "G. C. Howard wrote most of the songs, adding new ones as the play extended its New York run" (Railton).

5. Critique on Uncle Tom's Cabin

Uncle Tom's Cabin was a very controversial book when it was published in 1852. With her first antislavery novel, Stowe evoked "some of the liveliest and most distinguished criticism in American literature" (Ammons xvii). Some people praised it to heaven, others regarded it as a harsh attack on Southerners. People like George F. Holmes, a professor of history and literature, were of the opinion that Stowe intermeddled with things which didn't concern her at all (Holmes 8). As she made for raised tempers and stormy reactions among the people, it was not by chance that Abraham Lincoln greeted her as the lady who caused the Civil War. She certainly wasn't responsible for that alone, and didn't intend to insult and criticize Southern slaveholders, but rather the system itself. However, she made the people reflect on the political and social circumstances more closely, and thus stirred them up against one another.

5.1. The North

Apart from the mixed reactions concerning the content of the novel and the debate on slavery as well as Stowe's intention, a universal impression was that almost everyone read the book. "Ralph Waldo Emerson would later say that *Uncle Tom's Cabin* 'encircled the globe, and was the only book that found readers in the parlor, the nursery, and the kitchen'" (Gossett 165). John Greenleaf Whittier spoke of *Uncle Tom's Cabin* being an "immortal book" (Ammons (2007) 4). The book was unquestionably extremely popular. It appealed to the universal heart and moved its readers deeply, even made them cry. George Sand, the most popular female novelist of France, praised Stowe for having penetrated the hearts of the people "with emotions so sad and yet so sweet" (Sand 3). A problem was that such emotional responses to the book often tended to weaken its antislavery message. Many readers were "more impressed by the scenes in which little Eva appeared than they were by the novel's opposition to slavery." The famous abolitionist Wendell Phillips criticized that a lot of people loved the novel, but didn't abandon their proslavery principles at all. As far as the character of Eva is concerned, George F. Holmes also criticized that she wasn't original but nearly a copy of Charles Dickens' Little Nell (Holmes 15).

William Lloyd Garrison, the leading abolitionist of the North, gave *Uncle Tom's Cabin* a qualified endorsement. However, he wasn't too happy about the book. For one thing, his opposition to the "peculiar institution" went unrecorded in Stowe's novel. Abolitionist attitudes were assigned to the Quakers and other ordinary people instead. For another thing, the novel contained some ideas which Garrison strongly opposed, especially the idea of colonization – in her book, Stowe suggested that the blacks should emigrate to Africa. "It was the colonization arguments of *Uncle Tom's Cabin* which came closest to causing some abolitionists ... to reject the novel altogether" (Gossett 16870).

From her fellow writers, Stowe received positive and negative feedback for her bestseller. While Emerson, Whittier and Longfellow praised her for having written a brilliant book, other American writers of that time, with Hawthorne, Whitman, Melville and Thoreau leading the way, cared little for the book. Either they didn't mention it or they criticized it. "What might have repelled the other writers most of all was the perfervid religion espoused by the author and by some of the novel's characters" (Gossett 16567). Lydia Maria Child had problems with the religious aspects of the book, too.

The colonization theme which bothered Garrison also annoyed black abolitionists in the North. Furthermore, they were disturbed by the extreme softness of Uncle Tom. Although he disliked some passages of the book, especially the chapter about colonization – later he would tell Stowe that it was unlikely that blacks would earnestly wish to emigrate to Africa and leave the United States behind – Frederick Douglass found praising words for *Uncle Tom's Cabin*. "'The word of Mrs. Stowe is addressed to the soul of universal humanity,' he said." Nevertheless, many black critics deemed the character of Uncle Tom too submissive and pious, and found him a bad model for a black hero. They saw George Harris as the real hero of the book and admired him far more than they did Uncle Tom. Some black critics however, who rejected the book as a whole, went so far as to say that Stowe knew nothing about the black people and did not have any sympathy for them

(Gossett 17174).

Northern clergymen often spoke in favor of *Uncle Tom's Cabin* and praised Stowe as a genius. It was argued that the book had such a great success only because of its religious content. "... *Uncle Tom's Cabin* strongly appealed to the public, not principally because it was antislavery, but because it was Christian." As far as the theme of slavery was concerned, they liked the idea of colonization. Admittedly, they spoke out against slavery, but they were not in favor of blacks staying in the United States. In spite of some clergymen praising the book, others disliked it and found harsh critique. The editor of a conservative Presbyterian journal refered to the novel as "'antiChristian'" and "'antiministerial'". He felt the book to be an attack on ministers and churches. Again, the reactions were mixed and extremely oppositional (Gossett 17678).

Many people in the North were horrified by Stowe's advocacy of defying the law. In *Uncle Tom's Cabin* she clearly encouraged people to disobey the Fugitive Slave Law. George F. Holmes harshly criticized the character of Mr. Bird who helped Eliza to escape and thereby violated the law, even though he was in the position of a senator (Holmes 11). In the view of lawabiding people, this was a scandal. Hostile reviewers were also bothered about Stowe claiming freedom for the blacks without bearing in mind that they wouldn't know how to use their freedom. Finally, even reviewers who praised the book didn't think of it having any deep effect upon the debate on slavery. It was argued that *Uncle Tom's Cabin* wouldn't help enlarging the antislavery vote (Gossett 17981).

Political leaders of antislavery parties in the north found only little use for the novel in their appeals to voters before the Civil War. In their opinion, *Uncle Tom's Cabin* was too radical. Abraham Lincoln is said to have never read it. His eventual "changes in attitude toward slavery came largely from sources other than *Uncle Tom's Cabin*" (Gossett 182/83).

5.2. The South

The reactions to *Uncle Tom's Cabin* in the South were quite different. Most of the people were outraged and boilt with indignation. Those who liked the book and found praising words for it tried to remain anonymous. Defenders of slavery blamed Stowe for not depicting the truth and unfairly accentuating the evils of slavery. George F. Holmes was convinced, based on references to the laws by which slavery was regulated in the South, that many of Stowe's accusations towards the South were false. He suggested to Stowe who liked to refer to the bible, "'THOU SHALT NOT BEAR FALSE WITNESS AGAINST THY NEIGHBOR'" (Holmes22/24). The people didn't see that she was actually attacking the institution of slavery, not slaveholders themselves. In reaction to the widespread praise of the novel in the North, anger rose among Southerners. (Gossett 18589).

A crucial point of criticism was that Stowe as a woman publicly discussed sexual evils in her book. Especially women themselves were enraged, and condemned that as they thought that it was inappropriate. Southern reviewers were also furious about Stowe's advocacy of the defiance of law in *Uncle Tom's Cabin*. With Senator Bird and his wife helping Eliza to escape to Canada, she annoyed the people in the South. A. Beatty, a slaveholder from Missouri expressed what many other people thought. "She 'certainly knows that when white men – whether Quakers or no – help fugitive slaves, they are accessories in a murder, when an owner or his agent is killed.'" Furthermore, it was harshly criticized that Stowe didn't depict most of the blacks inferior to the white race, but partly even superior. Another point of criticism was that Stowe focused on the separation of black families being the worst evil. Reviewers admitted that it was true that separations happened from time to time, but they strongly emphasized that they occurred less often than the people in the North supposed. As far as whippings were concerned they said the same. Excessive maltreatments were rather unusual and didn't happen very often (Gossett 19194, 206).

Southern reviewers often disliked the white characters in *Uncle Tom's Cabin*. They were of the opinion that Stowe meant to defame the South by depicting the whites like she did. That she intended to criticize slavery as an institution by making Legree, by far the worst character of the novel, a Northerner, didn't occur to them. Augustine St. Clare was sometimes disliked even more for his easy way of life and his status as a gentleman. His arguments against slavery were often ridiculed. Mrs. Shelby didn't come off well, either. She was seen as one of the most unconvincing characters, but as contrasted with her, Marie St. Clare in fact enraged the people. Many women in the South felt insulted and said that ladies would never be like her. On the whole, to the opinion of the reviewers, the white slaveholders were portrayed too brutal. They devaluated scenes of cruelty and deemed them unpersuasive (Gossett 196200). George F. Holmes can well understand the Southerners disliking the white characters and feeling insulted. "... Mrs. Stowe ... is unable to look upon a white face without tracing in it something sinister and repulsive," he writes in his critical essay. Compared with the white characters, the Negro characters would be presented in a very positive light. "The negro under her brush invariably becomes handsome in person or character, or in both ...," he continues (Ammons 13).

"While the white characters in *Uncle Tom's Cabin* seemed openly offensive to southern reviewers, the black characters seemed merely unreal." Slaveholders said that there were no Uncle Tom's in the South, that his character was definitely exaggerated and, therefore, unconvincing. Topsy's credibility was often not denied, but she was rarely mentioned. Eliza and George Harris, the mulattoes of the novel, were the most objectionable. Reviewers thought that they were depicted as being too intelligent (Gossett 20205).

Another crucial point of criticism among Southerners was that *Uncle Tom's Cabin* advocated racial amalgamation and intermarriage. Surprisingly, some people admitted that under the conditions of slavery, sexual relations between white slaveholders and black slaves might be common (Gossett 205/06).

People from the South were mainly of the opinion that Stowe had given a false impression of what slavery was like. They felt like victims of a defaming and didn't understand that Stowe's aim was merely to criticize slavery as an institution, not people personally. Therefore, they became more and more angry with the Northerners.

5.3. AntiUncle Tom Literature

In response to *Uncle Tom's Cabin* many writers, whether from the North or – as in the majority of cases – from the South, wrote and published antiUncle Tom novels in which they depicted slavery as positive. According to Joy JordanLake, more than thirty novels were produced in direct response to Stowe's masterpiece, but the count varies from scholar to scholar

(JordanLake xvii). The antiUncle Tom novels defended the "peculiar institution" simply by a close reading of the Constitution as well as the Bible. The cruelties of slavery were mostly ignored. These works were sometimes almost identical with proslavery pamphlets. "Just as Stowe had done in *Uncle Tom's Cabin*, nearly all the authors of antiUncle Tom literary works adopted the convention of direct address to the reader … ." The main character of the antiUncle Tom novels was the tender and caring patriarchal slavemaster. Whippings were scarcely described. "When cruelties to slaves are shown in antiUncle Tom literature, they are the result of the personal defects of particular masters or, in rare instances, of mistresses." Noteworthy antiUncle Tom novels are Mary H. Eastman's *Aunt Phillis' Cabin* (1852), Maria J. McIntosh's *The Lofty and the Lowly* (1853), W. L. G. Smith's *Life at the South* (1852), and Baynard R. Hall's *Frank Freeman's Barber Shop* (1852) (Gossett 21217). Eastman's *Aunt Phillis' Cabin* sold about 18.000 copies within a few weeks. It was the first and most widely read proslavery response to *Uncle Tom's Cabin* (JordanLake 64).

6. Content of Uncle Tom's Cabin

Before the comparison of Stowe's novel and George Aiken's adaptation, the main part of this paper, the original plot of *Uncle Tom's Cabin* will be summed up to give an overview of the important characters and events.

Uncle Tom has been a servant on Arthur Shelby's farm in Kentucky for many years. The relationship between the slaveowner and his slaves has always been good, Shelby and his wife are caring parents to their "children". Never thought that it would ever happen, Shelby is forced by debt to sell his faithful, old slave Tom together with Harry, the little son of Eliza, a young quadroon on the Shelby plantation. Before Haley, the slavetrader, can take away his new possession, Harry is lost. His mother heard of the discussion and ran away with her baby in despair. The catch of Eliza and Harry fails when she crosses the Ohio River. Haley leaves for New Orleans without the boy. Two slavecatchers he met in a tavern agreed to take up pursuit of him and his mother. In case of a successful tracking, they would retain Eliza.

In the meantime, George Harris, Eliza's husband, has just escaped from his cruel master. Discovering that his wife has run away, too, and is headed for Canada, he sets out to find her. The young family is reunited at the house of a Quaker family which supported Eliza after she had crossed the Ohio River, and together they plan the next stage of their escape to freedom.

By that time, Tom travels down the Mississippi. On the river boat, he meets Eva, a little girl, who is accompanied by her father and her aunt Ophelia from Vermont on her way back home to New Orleans. She touches him deeply by her beauty and amiability. When she falls into the water, Tom rescues her, and is bought by her father Augustine St. Clare immediately. He is brought to his new home. Tom and Eva become good friends. They are connected with each other due to their Christian belief and their strong faith in God.

On their journey to Canada, Eliza and George are overtaken by the slavecatchers Loker and Marks. George defends his family successfully with the help of the Quaker Phineas. Their pursuers being wounded or having run away, the fugitives can proceed.

Back in New Orleans, St. Clare gives a slave girl to his sister Ophelia to raise. At the beginning, Ophelia is unable to cope with the wickedness of Topsy. She can't desist from her prejudices towards black people. Tom, who has been doing a good job managing his new master's household, is happy about the regular meetings for Bible study with Eva. He feels good at his new place, and is treated very well by his kind master, but he longs to be free and to return to his wife Chloe. St. Clare writes a letter to her to tell her about her husband's wellbeing.

Tom's family and the Shelbys are glad to hear the good news about Tom. Chloe makes her plan to work and save her wages to finally buy Tom's freedom. George Shelby already makes his plans about bringing Tom home.

After two years with the St. Clare family, it becomes apparent to Tom that his little friend Eva is incurably ill and will die soon. In the days before her death, Eva touches the hearts of all the people around her, and even succeeds in changing Topsy and encouraging her to be a better girl. She also has a good influence on Ophelia who begins to love Topsy. On the deathbed of his beloved daughter, St. Clare promises to give Tom his freedom, but when he is killed all of a sudden, his heartless and selfish wife Marie decides to sell all the slaves. Ophelia tries to change her mind, but doesn't succeed in saving the servants from being sold. Fortunately, she had made her brother sign Topsy over to her before his death.

At the slave warehouse in New Orleans, Tom besides two slave women, the one named Emmeline, is bought by Simon Legree and immediately taken to the rundown plantation of this cruel man. Tom´s new task is to pick cotton. Overworked and maltreated by the overseers Sambo and Quimbo, he only remains strong through his faith in God. Being in exuberant spirits, Legree strives for breaking Tom. Cassy, Legree´s black mistress, tries to help Tom by exerting influence on Legree.

At about the same time, Eliza and George make their way into freedom when crossing the Lake Erie into Canada. They´ve achieved their aim at last.

Tom, although prostrated, helps Cassy and Emmeline to escape. He also tries to arouse the Christian belief in his fellow servants. When Tom refuses to tell Legree what he knows about Cassy´s plan, Legree, having been driven mad by his former mistress, has Tom whipped to death. In his dying hour, Tom forgives Legree and the overseers for what they´ve done. George Shelby, who finally came to buy Tom´s freedom, comes too late to help his old friend. After a fight, Legree allows George Shelby to bury Tom. Sambo and Quimbo help him with that.

In the meantime, Cassy and Emmeline have made their escape. On a river boat they meet George Shelby and a lady. Cassy listens to their conversation and recognizes that the lady´s brother is the husband of her own daughter: Eliza. Together the women go to Canada to find their family members; someday the whole family goes to Europe, and finally plans to emigrate to Liberia. Topsy, having become a Christian and having lived with Ophelia for several years, would emigrate to Africa, too, to work as a missionary.

When George Shelby returns to Kentucky, he frees all his slaves. Tom´s cabin should always remind them of the man they owe their freedom to.

7. Comparison of Stowe´s Novel and Aiken´s Drama[2]

In the following main part of this paper, it will be the aim to compare the novel with its popular adaptation by Aiken according to the structure, the plot itself, the constellation of the characters as well as the presentation of them, and the themes. Which scenes or characters were left out or added by Aiken, which characters were presented in a different light, which themes were

---

2 The main part of this paper was worked on almost completely independently. Nearly no literature was used due to there being only very little about this specific topic.

emphazised, which aspects were taken over, and finally why all that – all this will be analyzed.

One mustn´t forget that Stowe and Aiken had a different audience in mind when writing the novel, respectively, the drama. At that time, in the middle of the nineteenth century, it was still mainly women reading novels and being addressed in them. Because of that, Stowe herself was of the opinion that in the case of *Uncle Tom´s* Cabin it wouldn´t be different (Wurst 2451). Especially sentimental novels were very popular evoking emotions and directly appealing to the hearts of the readers, making them feel for certain characters and even identify with them, and, on the other hand, despise other characters. Stowe´s novel clearly shows features of a sentimental novel. The author again and again addresses the readers directly, makes them put themselves into the situation of one of the characters, e.g. into the situation of Eliza when she´s about to lose her beloved child and in despair, and thereby suffer with them. All this was definitely not Aiken´s intention. His drama was not primarily addressed to women, but to men. In the course of the nineteenth century, American drama and theatre had become a commercial affair and a place of public controversy and emotional conflicts. It experienced a real boom by 1850. Theatre was not only for the elite anymore. As a form of mass entertainment, it addressed a popular audience – at that time primarily men. Aiken´s aim was to entertain his audience, making it laugh and have fun on the one hand, and trying to teach it and making it reflect on certain things on the other hand. People going to the theater wanted to have a nice evening and enjoy the play, but mostly not a play without any claim. Since theater reflected the American culture and history, social issues played a central role that provided for personal reflection and public discussion. Having a different audience in mind is definitely and unavoidably a reason for there being some differences between the novel and the drama. No matter whether both Stowe and Aiken wanted to earn money with their work, please their addresses, and express their social criticism – their addresses were not the same. This is an important point that shouldn´t be neglected.

There are people who say that Aiken´s stage version of *Uncle Tom´s Cabin* just like all the other versions is a mere copy of Stowe´s novel, that all the ideas are taken over and nearly no own ideas and themes incorporated. This is hard to believe if one bears in mind that Aiken had started to write his drama before Stowe finished with the final version of her novel and published it in book form. Other adaptations of *Uncle Tom's Cabin* were put on stage even earlier in 1852. Of course, it is right that Stowe's novel was the model for the stage versions of *Uncle Tom's Cabin*, that her characters and themes were used more or less, but actually everyone bringing a play to the stage changed something, left something out or added something in order to achieve certain effects and switch the focus on aspects more important to him. No matter whether Aiken's version is said to come closest to Stowe's novel, he still incorporated his own ideas. It would be wrong to suppose that Aiken simply copied Stowe's novel, and in the following section this will be brought out.

7.1. Structure and Plot

The novel consists of fortyfive chapters all in all, including the concluding remarks, in which Stowe talks about the authenticity of her novel, and addresses both Northerners and Southerners in a critical voice talking about the wrongs of the institution of slavery and the lack of reflexion and social action among the American people. The focus of the narrative as well as the characters switch from chapter to chapter due to there being actually two plots: the plot of Eliza and that of Uncle Tom. The advantage of having these two plots is that both the attitudes toward slavery in the North and in the South can be explored (Gossett 101).

Aiken's play consists of six acts, each act itself consisting of four to six scenes. All in all, there are thirty scenes. While Stowe focuses on the plantation owner Arthur Shelby in the first chapter of the novel, Aiken focuses on Eliza and her husband George, the two mulattoes, respectively quadroons of the story. That Aiken chose the dialogue between these two characters for the first scene of his play certainly had a specific reason. Right from the start the audience is induced to be sympathetic to the two slaves who would break the laws of the country later on. As Eliza and George are only lightskinned and welleducated, the audience can identify itself more easily. In the novel, the dialogue between George and Eliza can be found in the third chapter.

The second chapter of the novel is about Eliza, the title is "The Mother." In this chapter one learns about Eliza's and George's past and present situation, about their marriage. The readers are induced to suffer with Eliza and feel for her. While in Stowe's novel the focus lies on Eliza, Aiken in his drama puts George in the center of attention. This chapter was omitted by him.

The fourth chapter of the novel can't be found in the novel, either. In this chapter, one learns a lot about Uncle Tom and his family. Detailed pieces of information are given. A main difference between a novel and a drama is that while in a novel there is a narrator, in a drama there is none who can give additional pieces of information or evaluative comments, there are only the dialogues and a few stage directions and authorial comments. It's mostly up to the audience of a play to form an opinion and make judgements according to what is seen on the stage, how certain characters behave. Gestures and mimic play an important role, too.

Besides the chapters two and four, several other chapters were omitted by Aiken. This, among other things, has to do with the deliberate selection of characters for the drama, which will be analyzed further in 7.2.. Having a look at the first ten chapters of the novel and comparing it with the drama, one finds out that except for the first and the third chapter, only the chapters seven and eight play a role in the drama. In these chapters, there is one climax of the story: Eliza crosses the Ohio River by jumping from ice floe to ice floe to escape her pursuers who want to take her son Harry away from her (1,5/6). The content of all the other chapters doesn't play any role at all. Neither the dialogue between Mr. and Mrs. Shelby, nor the involvement of the Shelby slaves Sam and Andy in the pursuit of Eliza, nor the scene with Senator Bird and his wife is included in the drama. Except for leaving out several chapters, Aiken put some of the scenes in another order. In his drama, Haley does business with the slavecatchers Loker and Marks before Eliza crosses the river. In the novel, it's the other way around. To sum it up, the content of the chapters one, three, seven, and eight, corresponds with the five scenes of the first act of the drama.

Scene 2,1 of the drama starts out with Tom having arrived at his new master's house in New Orleans. St. Clare's whole family is introduced. In Stowe's novel, these characters don't play any role until chapter fourteen. Chapter fifteen corresponds with the opening scene of the second act of the drama. In 2,2, Topsy appears for the first time. In the novel, she is introduced not before chapter twenty. Stowe, before focusing on the St. Clare family, described Tom's way down the Mississippi and what occurred on the river boat in detail. All this was left out by Aiken. The content of the chapters eleven and thirteen, in which George and Eliza are foregrounded and one learns about George's escape and what happened to Eliza after she had crossed the Ohio River, corresponds with scene 2,3 and 2,5 of the drama. In 2,6, George and Eliza make their last appearance, when they escape Loker and Marks with the help of Phineas. This scene can be found in chapter seventeen in the novel. In the last four acts of the drama, George and Eliza don't play any role any more. The focus lies on Tom and Eva on the one hand, and on the new plot with the characters Gumption Cute and Deacon Perry on the other hand.

While in the drama, there is a binary division as far as the two main plots of the original story are concerned, – in the first two acts Eliza and George play a central role, in the other four acts they don't appear any more and the focus lies on Uncle Tom – in the novel, there is a tripartite division. At the beginning, George and especially Eliza are in the center of attention. In the middle section, they nearly don't play any role at all, remain unmentioned for nineteen chapters at a stretch. Uncle Tom is foregrounded. After his death in chapter fourtyone, Eliza and George appear again, and one learns what happened to them after their escape to Canada.

The third act of the drama covers the incidents at the St. Clare household up to little Eva's death in 3,6. This central passage of the drama matches the central chapters twentytwo and twentyfour to twentysix of the novel – chapter twentythree about Eva and her cousin Henrique didn't find any use in the drama. Aiken, however, partly chose another order, and the scene in which Eva tells Topsy that she loves her even appears as early as in scene 2,4.

The fourth act of the drama, at least the scenes 4,2/4,4 fit together with the chapters twentyseven and twentyeight of the novel. The occurences up to the death of St. Clare are covered. In 4,1, Aiken's added character Gumption Cute makes his first appearance. This scene marks the beginning of a new plot.

The new plot with Topsy, Ophelia, and the two added characters Cute and Deacon develops in the next act. Half of the scenes covers Ophelia being much courted. The other two scenes deal with Tom being sold and the first occurrences at Legree's plantation. These scenes match chapter thirty and chapter thirtytwo of the novel. Chapter twentynine about the happenings in New Orleans immediately after St. Clare's death as well as chapter thirtyone in which one learns about Legree's attitudes towards his slaves is left out.

For his final act, Aiken added three and part of a fourth scene of the six scenes all by himself. In 6,2, George Shelby bursts upon Marks, who tells him about what happened in New Orleans and says that he'll lead him to Legree's plantation. In 6,4, Marks has a conversation with Gumption Cute about blackmailing Legree. The next scene includes the two of them having a fight with Tom's third master. For his final scene, Aiken let Eva appear like an angel in heaven being united with Uncle Tom and her father St. Clare. The third main episode of the original story about Tom staying with his new master Legree, was to a large extent neglected by Aiken. Altogether, he excluded the content of five chapters dealing with the occurrences at Legree's plantation. In the last act of the drama, only a few things are included. In 6,1 Tom talks to Cassy after having been beaten up – but the dialogue between the two of them is shortened. 6,3 matches chapter thirtyfive of the novel. Having a conversation with Cassy, Legree is brought a lock of hair by Sambo and feels haunted. Scene 6,5 finally covers the death of Uncle Tom.

As George and Eliza make their last appearance at the end of the second act in the drama, the content of the last four chapters of the novel is omitted. All those coincidences toward the end of the story don't play any role. The novel ends with George and Eliza being reuinted with the rest of their family and emigrating to Liberia after they didn't play any role in the central chapters of the novel. The drama, however, ends with the death of Uncle Tom.

7.2. Characters

All in all, Aiken took over many of Stowe's characters, especially the main characters, but he presented some of them in a different way, left out some characters which play an important role in the novel, and added a few.

7.2.1. Characters Left Out by Aiken

It is conspicuous that Aiken left out mainly female characters. Neither Mrs. Bird nor Mrs. Shelby appear in the drama. In Stowe's novel, however, they are of great importance. Mrs. Shelby and Mrs. Bird are presented as morally superior compared to their husbands. They are quite powerful and have a strong influence on their husbands. Mrs. Shelby provides for the pursuit of Eliza and Harry not being successful by making plans with her slaves to whom she has a very good relationship and who have to take part in the pursuit of their friend. She is the one who reproaches Arthur Shelby for selling Tom and reminds him of his promise to free him. She is a religious person and actually an opponent of slavery, but she seems to be forced into the situation of having slaves in Kentucky (Gossett 115). To her husband she says, "I was a fool to think I could make anything good out of such a deadly evil. It is a sin to hold slaves under laws like ours ... I thought by kindness, and care, and instruction, I could make the condition of mine better than freedom – fool that I was!" In response to that, Arthur Shelby, who accepts the moral and spiritual superiority of his wife, says, "Why, wife, you are getting to be an abolitionist, quite!" (Stowe (1967) 42). Mrs. Shelby's relationship to her slaves is rather that of a mother to her children. In the fifth chapter she says, "O, Mr. Shelby, I have tried ... to do my duty to these poor, simple, dependent creatures. I have cared for them, instructed them, watched over them, and known all their little cares and joys, for years ..." (Stowe (1967) 41).

Mrs. Bird is another female character in the novel who cares for the slaves and puts her moral laws over those of the country. She is an abolitionist. On her escape to Canada, Eliza meets Mrs. Bird and her husband. Deeply touched by what Eliza tells her, Mrs. Bird makes her husband help her, although he as a senator voted in favor of the Fugitive Slave Act. Nevertheless, his wife has such a strong influence on him that he breaks his oath and the law of the country in favor of the moral law and his reason, and helps Eliza. That Aiken did not only leave out the character of Mrs. Bird, but also that of her husband, has probably to do with the fact that this character as a politician broke the laws of his country which was a real scandal. Stowe was harshly criticized for this passage in her novel. No matter whether Aiken knew about that or not, he obviously tried to avoid attacking the advocates of slavery too directly and encouraging people to disregard the law in favor of the slaves. The characters of Mrs. Bird and Mrs. Shelby contribute to making Stowe's novel a feminist text. It seems to be obvious that Aiken as a male playwright, who didn't have primarily women in mind as his addresses, didn't present this in his drama, that he refused to give the female characters so much power and rather omitted them.

Except for the mentioned female characters, Mrs. Shelby and Mrs. Bird, and the character of Mr. Bird, Aiken omitted several other minor male and female characters. The reason for that might be that these characters aren't that important, don't impel the plot, and the play would have boosted out had Aiken integrated all of them. They wouldn't have been necessary in the play. Stowe certainly had something specific in mind when letting certain characters appear. Chapter twentythree, e.g., is about Henrique, Eva's cousin who visits her one day together with his father Alfred, St. Clare's brother. In this passage, Stowe clearly presents the evil of slavery, the danger that someone has so much power over another human being that he cannot control it. Henrique sees his slave Dodo merely as a thing, whips him and insults him arbitrarily. He doesn't really understand why Eva criticizes him because of that, and how she can think that the black slaves are equal to her. Eva behaves like a person free from prejudices and condemnations, who embodies human love. In chapter thirty, Stowe lets Emmeline appear together with her mother Susan. They are to be sold at an auction together with the slaves of the St. Clare estate. In this passage, Stowe shows the in her opinion worst evil of slavery: the separation of families. Susan, having always been afraid of being parted from her daughter one day, now has to face this situation when Legree refuses to take her to his plantation, too, and is despaired and shattered. In this passage, Stowe gets very sentimental and again appeals to the hearts of her readers. In the whole novel there are many scenes like the mentioned one showing the interaction between the slaves, giving an insight into their lives and feelings. Aiken cut several of them. He was "highly selective in what he included" (Gardner 167). And obviously, he didn't include a lot of scenes in which the slaves interact, in which one learns about their personal relationships, scenes, which are to some extend sentimental like e.g. the scene in which Emmeline is separated from her mother, or the scene in which one learns about Uncle Tom's family life. As a result, characters like Sam and Andy, the two slaves of Shelby, who in the novel trick Haley to help their fellow Eliza escape, Mose and Pete, the sons of Uncle Tom, and Dinah, Rosa and Mammy, the slaves of St. Clare, don't play any role in the drama. Aiken only focused on the main slave characters, namely Tom, Topsy, George and Eliza.

Another group of characters, Aiken didn't take over from the novel except for the character of Phineas Fletcher, are the activists for the "underground railroad", primarily Simeon and Rachel Halliday, Mrs. Smyth and Mr. Symmes. The "underground railroad" was a prearranged route along which runaway slaves could be passed to Canada. "Thomas Garrett, a Delaware Quaker (later the original for Simeon Halliday in *Uncle Tom's Cabin*), was said to have aided more than 2,700 fugitive slaves before being apprehended in 1848" (Filler 329).

7.2.2. Characters Added by Aiken

To put his own stamp on the drama, Aiken, except for leaving out wellselected characters from the novel, added a few characters to the story which he invented all by himself. These are the characters of Gumption Cute and Deacon Perry. To broaden the humor in his play, Aiken included the character of Gumption Cute, "a laughable loser" (Richards 370) and "hapless vagabond" (Gardner 167), who competes for Ophelia's affections with his rival Deacon Perry. With the two of them, Aiken adds a completely new plotline to the original story. Cute, once an overseer on a cotton plantation, lost his job and lots of money in a bad speculation. He wants to find Ophelia in Vermont, whom he claims to be a rich relative, and seriously calculates on money. In Vermont he meets Deacon Perry who lost his wife and has made up his mind about having Ophelia as his new partner. He tries to win her heart. Ophelia feels flattered by Perry and in the end decides to marry him. Cute is thrown out of the house – Ophelia thinks that he´s only after her money. In the last act of the play Cute appears again in a scene that isn´t presented in the novel. Together with Marks he plans to blackmail Legree to get money. The two of them witnessed Legree killing St. Clare in a quarrel in New Orleans. In a final fight with them, Legree dies.

7.2.3. Characters in Both the Novel and the Drama

Topsy and Ophelia

By adding this new plotline with the characters of Gumption Cute and Deacon Perry to the story, Aiken additionally provided for the characters of Ophelia and Topsy to accept new traits. These two characters show the greatest tranformation from the novel to the drama of all major characters. In the drama, Ophelia is reduced to a "cardboard spinster (who says the word ´shiftless` too many times to count)" (Gardner 167). The character of Topsy "is greatly foregrounded and expanded" (Gardner 168). "While some of the dialogue is quite like that of the novel, Aiken´s character also dances a breakdown and becomes a thoroughly theatrical character – one very near a minstrel ´darky`" (Richards 370). In their first conversation, when he is told her name, Cute accuses Topsy of being "a juvenile specimen of Day & Martin", a "blackface minstrel act of the period" (Richards 511). When Ophelia in the end wants him to leave immediately, Topsy has a funny performance. She beats Cute with a broom around stage making him look like a fool. In the drama, Topsy´s character is definitely drawn more comically, especially in all those scenes which Aiken invented all by himself. In the other scenes her character comes close to that of the novel, the dialogues are the same except for a few less remarkable variations and omissions. The stereotypical clashing between her and Ophelia at the beginning is presented well by Aiken as well as stereotypical black habits like singing, dancing, stealing, lying, being silly and trying to imitate white people. With his play, Aiken primarily wanted to entertain his audience.

Especially with his new plotline and the nearly exaggerated characters of Ophelia and Topsy, who thinks she'll be turned into "a little brack angel" after her death, he could easily come up to the expectations of the audience that also wanted funny scenes and exceptional performances to laugh about.

St. Clare and his family

The characters of Augustine St. Clare and his family are taken over by Aiken, too, but at least the characters of him and his wife Marie aren't transformed that much. Marie remains the selfish, invalid and selfpitiful southern belle of the novel, but her character is simply not drawn as cruel and coldhearted as in the novel. Stowe described her character in detail, focused on her only in chapter sixteen and let her appear in several other chapters. Marie is characterized as being jealous of her daughter for attracting the attention of all the others to herself. She doesn't care for her daughter when she's incurably ill, and after her death she even sees herself as the greatest sufferer and reproaches her husband whom she always criticizes and treats rather badly. After her husband's sudden death she doesn't mourn for a long time, but quickly provides for the house and most of the servants of St. Clare to be sold at an auction. In this scene she is presented extremely coldhearted when she doesn't consent to Ophelia's request to free Tom what St. Clare had promised him to do before he died. In another passage, Marie is presented as being very racist. Having been asked by Eva for what reason she keeps slaves she says, "I don't know, I'm sure, except for a plague; they are the plague of my life. I believe that more of my ill health is caused by them than by any one thing; and ours, I know, are the very worst that ever anybody was plagued with." Inspite of her saying that, she actually likes the servants to be around her, paying all their attention to her. On the whole, Marie is presented as "unthinkingly heartless but too indolent to be aggressively cruel" (Adams 51). In Aiken's drama, Marie appears only in two scenes. When her husband and Eva return from Vermont with Ophelia she welcomes them with statements about her bad health. St. Clare is reproached for having written only short letters. In the dramatical scene of Eva's death, Marie is presented as if she hadn't known about her daughter's illness at all and is totally shocked when she's about to die. For his presentation of Marie, Aiken was very likely not criticized unlike Stowe who was harshly attacked by many women from the South saying that they wouldn't be like that (Gossett 200).

That he focused on her only in passing gives the impression that the character of Marie was of no great importance for Aiken. Furthermore, by leaving out the scene in which Marie talks to Ophelia about selling the slaves, Aiken avoids the discussion of sectional issues. The clash between the southern belle Marie and the Northerner Ophelia, who wants slavery to be abolished, isn´t presented.

In opposition to the character of Marie, the character of Augustine St. Clare is of greater importance for Aiken. He appears in several scenes, most of the important dialogues from the novel are taken over by Aiken, and his character isn´t really transformed. In Stowe´s novel he is presented as a rich young man, openminded, and sometimes very sarcastic, but without doubt a friendly and polite person who treats his slaves very well, even indulges them for what he is criticized by his wife and sister. Wouldn´t it bring him so much wealth, he´d be an opponent of slavery as he sees the evils of the "peculiar institution." He loves his daughter Eva more than everything else in the world; his mother played an important role in his life, too, and influenced him a lot. Again Stowe shows the power of women and their moral superiority. It is remarkable that while in the drama St. Clare´s last words are "Eva, I come!", in the novel he exclaims *"Mother!"* before he dies. In the whole novel the role of the mother is emphasized. Aiken, however, put Eva into the center of attention. The two to Stowe´s opinion bad qualities of St. Clare are that he sometimes drinks too much alcohol and that he is an agnostic. As mentioned above, Aiken didn´t change very much as far as the character of Augustine St. Clare is concerned. However it´s interesting to see that he avoided the discussion of sectional issues by leaving out the long dialogue between him and his sister Ophelia about slavery again. This leads to the assumption that Aiken didn´t see slavery as a sectional, but rather as a national issue and therefore omitted too heavy clashes of Northerners and Southerners and their political attitudes. What Aiken at least included, is the dialogue between St. Clare and Ophelia about Eva and Tom. In this dialogue it becomes clear that Ophelia has prejudices towards black people, that she is an opponent of slavery, but actually doesn´t like them that much. St. Clare on the other hand has no problem at all with his daughter kissing Tom and her sitting on his knees. In the dialogue with his daughter, one learns that he has servants only for his convenience, but that he doesn´t support the system. The majority of the people in the theater might have been shocked to see little Eva kissing the "darky" Tom – to avoid that, Aiken had a white man only with his face painted black play the role of Uncle Tom.

The only female character in the play who really exerts influence on men is Eva. On the whole, she is presented quite similar compared with the novel. For Stowe, she serves as a vehicle to relate her religious and political ideas. "Politically, Eva represents the possibility that whites can recognize their shared humanity with those of African descent. Religiously, she embodies Christian love" (Shackelford 1227). Being only about six years old she is aware of the injustice and the evils of slavery. Sacrificially she provides for the servants of her parents to feel good supporting them whenever she can, always treating them as equal. Eva, the fragile angelic child, is the only character who is seriously able to totally transcend the racial barriers between black slaves and their white owners. She's extremely pious and even prays for her servants. Her Christian belief brings her close to Uncle Tom. They have their regular conversations about religion, and Eva reads to him in the Bible while Tom sings for her. She loves him and lets him know that. When she feels that she'll die soon she isn't unhappy, but talks with joy about heaven, the place she'll get to. She thinks that one must be a faithful Christian to get to heaven one day. Therefore, she teaches her servants to believe, tries to make Topsy a better person and a Christian, and endeavers to make her father believe in God, too. In the hour of death she advocates that her father gives Tom his freedom, and gives a curl of her hair to every slave so that they always remember her and her plea that they should be Christians. With that she mainly provides for Topsy changing completely and not being wicked any more. Ophelia is touched by her, too, and tries to do what Eva gladly did: to love Topsy. Eva shows that love is the highest law of all. She dies with her last words: "Oh! Love, joy, peace!" (Stowe 277). "With Eva, Stowe draws upon the Victorian sentimental tradition of children too good for a fallen world" (Shackelford 1228). The description of the moment of her death is supposed to have been similar to that of Stowe's mother (Gossett 143). In Aiken's play the character of Eva comes very close to that of the novel, but her dialogues are shortened or even left out. The scene in which she tells her servants to be Christians and gives each one of them a lock of her hair to remember her and what she said, is left out. This scene would probably have been too sentimental for Aiken's play, and it focused too much on Christian religion. As already mentioned, Aiken didn't put such a high emphasis on this topic in the whole play. To at least mention this scene, however, he has Topsy say what happened. Some other dialogues, e.g. that between her and Topsy, are taken over by Aiken. However, he somehow presented her as a "sugary little simpleton" and exaggerated her role (Gossett 130). Especially one scene of the play is remarkable, namely the final one. Aiken's play ends with Eva, robed in white, "on the back of a milkwhite dove, with expanded wings, as if just soaring upward. Her hands are extended in benediction over ST. CLARE and UNCLE TOM, who are kneeling and gazing up to her." This scene must have been very impressive for the audience, lights and music intensified the effect of the final scene. To have Eva appear in such a sublime position at the end of his play could suggest that Aiken wanted to emphasize the importance of love and humanity being above all. On the other hand it could simply be the case that he wanted to impress his audience with such an amazing final scene to top off an impressive and entertaining, but also thoughtprovoking play, and he left it to every single person to find an own interpretation for it. "An article in the 3 November 1853 *National Era*" suggests as a reason for having this scene as the final one that Aiken perhaps simply wanted to prevent "'the abrupt and disorderly departure of a portion of the audience amid [Tom's] deathscene, which characterized the finale heretofore.'" (Railton)

Uncle Tom

In Stowe's novel, Uncle Tom is presented as a large and powerful man, kind, benevolent, and with good sense. Although he is her strongest weapon against slavery (Gossett 102) and "the most significant character for exploring the institution of slavery", his role in the novel "is more strongly religious than political" (Shackelford 1230). For Stowe, he possessed all those religious traits she herself admired, he was "the perfect Christian" (Gossett 103). In Aiken's drama, religion plays an important role as well, but not nearly such a central one. What is more is that Christianity is questioned. Again, Aiken carefully selected the events and dialogues he included in his drama. On the whole, there aren't too many differences. When he's about to be sold and Eliza encourages him to try to escape, too, he doesn't want to do that. He says that he has never broken trust and won't do so. For him, his master Shelby is not to blame. He trusts in God and accepts his fate. What is left out by Aiken is the dialogue between Tom and Shelby in which Tom asks him whether he has done anything wrong for what he is now to be sold. A reason for Aiken omitting this dialogue could either be that it was too sentimental for his drama or that Aiken tried to not present Arthur Shelby as a humane and good slaveholder who was an innocent victim of the circumstances. In opposition to Stowe, Aiken didn't draw such a positive picture of Tom's first master and whitewash the fact that he sold his best and most faithful servant whom he had promised his freedom before.

While Stowe in her novel describes Tom's way down the Mississippi to New Orleans and the events that happen on board of the boat, Aiken leaves that out. At the beginning of the second act, one learns about Tom having rescued Eva from drowning and having been bought afterwards, when St. Clare tells his wife about their journey back home, but the story about the girl Lucy whose child Haley takes away to sell it and who as a result of that commits suicide is omitted. To Aiken, the relationship between the slaves as well as their very personal stories weren't important for his drama. Except for this passage, there were several others from the novel which he left out for this reason.

Tom's stay with St. Clare's family is presented very similarly both in the novel and in the drama, but in the latter the events are shortened. Tom and Eva are quite attached to one another. They are joined together through their Christian faith. While Tom sings for Eva, his little friend reads to him from the Bible. When Eva gets incurably ill, Tom is the first to be told that she feels she'll go to heaven soon. In this passage of the story, a short dialogue between Tom and Ophelia in which he tells her about what Eva told him is added by Aiken. When Eva dies, Tom is very sad, but also happy, because Eva is released from her physical and psychological pain and is in a better world where Jesus is. After her death Tom cares for his master St. Clare. He tries to be a spiritual adviser for him and help him become a believer – that was Eva's wish. St. Clare soon feels better and thinks that he's nearer to Eva. During his whole stay in New Orleans, Tom had been a caring, honest and faithful servant to his master. The dialogue in which he tells St. Clare that he doesn't want him to drink too much alcohol to be injurious to his health, in which there is a reference to the temperance movement of that time, is taken over by Aiken, too. He likes his master a lot and is treated well, but nevertheless, he has a desire for freedom. When St. Clare tells him that he'll make him a free man, he is very joyful to St. Clare's astonishment. To him he says, "I'd rather have poor clothes, poor house, poor everything, and have 'em *mine*, than have the best, if they belonged to somebody else. I had *so* mas'r; I think it's natur', mas'r" (Aiken 416). This dialogue is taken over from the novel as well. Tom, however, doesn't want to leave his master before he's become a believer. In the end Tom isn't released into freedom, when St. Clare all of a sudden is killed before signing the papers making Tom a free man. In this passage an important difference between the novel and the drama can be made out. While in Stowe's novel one gets the impression that Tom forgives his master for not having provided for him getting the papers in time when it is said that he "felt at peace about his master," in the drama, neither does Tom directly say that he forgives him nor does one learn about his feelings later on. There is no hint for Tom's forgiveness. This leads to the assumption that the fact that St. Clare was careless and forgot to sign the papers making Tom a free man, why Tom is now unprotected and handed over to the will of St. Clare's cruel wife Marie, is something that simply can't be forgiven for Aiken. Just like Arthur Shelby, St. Clare, Tom's second master, isn't presented in such a positive light. It seems like Aiken tried to emphasize that every slaveowner no matter how kind and indulgent has his negative features and can't be completely good due to the "peculiar institution." The system of slavery is an evil which slaveowners are part of. It is only because of St. Clare's carelessness that Tom is sold to Simon Legree.

The last section of the novel is very much shortened by Aiken and there are some more differences. In the drama one doesn't really learn about what Tom has to do on Legree's plantation and what the plantation was like. One only learns that Tom has to live in a rude chamber and that he's come to "dark places" as he says himself. In opposition to that, Stowe gives a detailed description of everything. It is said that Tom has to work in the fields and pick cotton. Another scene left out by Aiken is the one in which Legree tells his new slaves that he doesn't want them to exercise their religion freely. This was probably superfluous for him as other scenes show Legree's repellant attitude toward religion. A difference between the novel and the drama can be made out in the scene in which Tom has to whip a fellow slave and resists to do so for what he is badly punished. While the dialogue between him and Legree is taken over by Aiken in which Tom says that he'd rather die than whip anyone, and that Legree would never possess his soul, the fellow slave who's supposed to be whipped is a different one. In the drama Legree wants Emmeline to be whipped when she resists giving him enough affection. In the novel, it is the girl Lucy who didn't pick enough cotton. She isn't mentioned at all in the drama. Her story seems to have been of no importance for Aiken. What's identical is that Cassy cares for Tom after his punishment, and that Tom tries to make her trust in God. In the drama, Tom doesn't lose his faith on Legree's plantation, but he doesn't gain new strength in his misery and doesn't feel that God is standing between him and Legree, either; he doesn't experience a victory. Still he forgives Legree and the overseers Sambo and Quimbo for what they've done, when he's about to die after having been beaten up. He was blamed for Cassy's escape and did not tell Legree anything. In opposition to the novel, it's not mentioned at all in the drama how Tom helped Cassy and Emmeline to excape. Neither is it mentioned that before her escape Cassy wanted Tom to kill Legree in his sleep what he refused to do. The reason for Tom forgiving those who fatally hurt him is the same in both the novel and the drama. Tom sees them as poor creatures, as victims themselves. Having taken this over, Aiken also tries to show that it's rather the system of slavery to be blamed for all the bad things that happen than the slave owners themselves. And one mustn't forget that Aiken presented Legree as a Northerner, too, to emphasize that it were not the people of the South who were to be attacked and criticized personally, but the system. While in the novel Tom is said to have gained a victory after the first time he was beaten up, why he was quite joyful from then on and tried to encourage his fellow slaves to escape, that his faith was tested and proved its worth, this is not the case in the drama. Only in the moment of death does Tom feel good again and sees that God has given him the victory. *"Heaven has come!"* In the novel Tom's Christian faith makes him strong in every situtation. In the drama, however, his religion is often questioned.

Simon Legree

"From Simon Legree´s first appearance in the novel at a slave auction, the reader senses that he is vile, repulsive, and sadistic" (Shackelford 1226/7). In Aiken´s play, Legree, Tom´s third master, is the same bad guy. He treats his slaves very badly, insults them, whips them and lets his overseers Sambo and Quimbo beat them up whenever he likes. He buys Emmeline to have a new younger mistress for his older mistress Cassy in whom he sees a devilish person, and Tom to do the hard work on his rundown plantation. When Emmeline doesn´t give him enough affection, Legree wants Tom to whip her, but he resists to do so and says that he´d rather die than hurt a fellow slave. From then on Legree hates Tom bitterly. When Sambo brings him a lock of hair he got from Tom, it seems that the tide is turned. Legree suddenly is afraid of Tom. The curl reminds him of his mother, who nearly made him a better person, but whom he left alone. When she died, he received a letter from her, in which she forgave him, together with a curl of her hair which he immediately burned to forget her. After the escape of Cassy and Emmeline, however, Legree is enraged again. He blames Tom for everything and injures him fatally. Legree finally dies in a fight with Cute and Marks who wanted to blackmail him as they knew about Legree having killed St. Clare in New Orleans. Except for the final scene and Legree´s end, his role stays quite the same, the dialogues are to a great extend taken over by Aiken. He was the character the audience was supposed to feel antipathy for, the cruel master. It is a little bit astonishing that Aiken also included the scene in which Legree is reminded of his mother and tells the story of his life. Other personal stories were completely left out or extremely shortened by Aiken. A reason for him including this scene could be that he wanted to present Legree not only as a bad guy, but also as a figure of fun, an idiot the audience could laugh at when the cruel master all of a sudden is afraid and gives in only because of a curl of hair. He primarily wanted to entertain his audience. This shouldn´t be neglected here. Furthermore, Eva´s curl has a symbolic character: it stands for humanity and Christian love. In this scene it could also show that even a man like Legree is not inhumane and devilish to the core, but that its the system of slavery that makes people turn into cruel people.

Cassy

The character of Cassy doesn´t play such an important role in Aiken´s drama. Cassy is Legree´s mistress who knows exactly about him being a cruel and coldhearted man since she has stayed with him for several years. She hates Legree and warns Tom of his new master. In this conversation one learns that Cassy has lost her faith in God. The only way for her to get out of her misery is to escape. Except for this scene, Aiken lets Cassy appear only in one other scene, in which she´s having a conversation with Legree. Here one learns that Legree is afraid of her. In the play, however, it´s not Cassy who makes Legree go mad in the end, but a lock which Sambo got from Tom. In Stowe´s novel Cassy is of greater importance. She appears in nearly every chapter from the thirtythird chapter onwards. One chapter is only about the story of her life, one gets lots of pieces of information about her. In another scene she warns Emmeline of Legree and prepares their escape to which even Tom encourages her and with which he helps her. With Cassy as the protagonist Stowe´s novel becomes a gothic novel in chapter fourtytwo. Hidden in the garret under Legree´s house she comes out at night to frighten Legree who is driven mad and in the end becomes an alcoholic. Cassy and Emmeline succeed in escaping from his plantation. After her escape Cassy is reunited with her family. With the character of Cassy, Stowe focused on the relationship between black slaves which Aiken omitted to a great extent. Furthermore, Stowe thematized the sexual relationship between a black slave mistress and her white master. In addition to that, Stowe appeals to hearts of her readers in the passage about the story of Cassy´s life. Again she presents the worst evil of slavery, the separation of families. Cassy has two children who were taken away from her and of whom she has never heard of again. Finally, Cassy is another strong and influential woman of the story. She has so much power that she even influences her cruel master. As mentioned above, the novel was seen as a feminist text. All this didn´t play any role for Aiken just like the final coincidences of the novel.

George and Eliza

Many of the passages from the novel in which Eliza and George appear are omitted by Aiken, especially those toward the end of the story. Nevertheless, the most remarkable events and dialogues are included in the drama. Aiken even chose the dialogue between Eliza and her husband George for the opening scene. In this scene one learns that George is desperate and angry about his master. He lost his job in a factory because of him, and was treated very badly. He seems rebellious saying straightforward that his master wouldn't have the right to be his master. Eliza wants him to calm down and trust in God, but George has already made his plans about fleeing to Canada, and says that he has lost his faith in a world where so many bad things happen. This dialogue can be found in the third chapter of the novel. In contrast to Aiken, Stowe emphasizes the religious remarks a bit more and uses the word "God" while Aiken uses "heaven." She had been a very faithful and pious woman for all her life, and had been educated in that way. Religion was a central part of her life. She believed in God and him doing good. We don't know what Aiken's religious conviction was. Maybe he tried to keep more distance in this point. For another reason it is remarkable, too, that Aiken leaves out one of the religious remarks of the novel. George's "Pray for me, Eliza, perhaps the good Lord will hear *you*." conveys the impression that George accepts a moral superiority of his wife. This submissiveness is not to be found in Aiken's drama. Right in the first scene Aiken shows clearly that the slaves of his drama don't just accept their lot, give in and be submissive towards their white masters, especially not George (Toll 90). This is a very important feature of the drama, and Aiken emphasizes it very often.

Although in a different order, the incidents at the beginning of the drama are almost the same. Eliza listens to a conversation between Mr. and Mrs. Shelby – this conversation is only mentioned in the drama – and learns that her son Harry will be sold. To prevent her son being taken away from her she plans to escape. Having talked to Chloe and Uncle Tom about what happened she runs away. The climax of Eliza's plot, the scene in which she crosses the Ohio River by jumping from ice floe to ice floe is taken over by Aiken. Some incidents, however, are different. While in the novel Haley hires Loker and Marks for the pursuit of Eliza after she crossed the Ohio River and while on the other side of the river Mr. Symmes helps her, in the drama Eliza listens to the conversation between Haley and the slavecatchers at the tavern and then crosses the river, and it's Phineas who is the white knight and helps her on both sides of the river. After this scene, Aiken doesn't focus on Eliza that much any more. She appears only in two other scenes in the second act and is rather passive. In opposition to her, George is foregrounded. The dialogue

44

between him and his former employer Wilson, who is presented similarly both in the novel and in the drama, at the tavern in which Wilson tries to keep him from running away and breaking the laws of the United States, is taken over by Aiken, at least the most important sentences. The passage in which George tells Wilson that he should find Eliza and tell her about his plans is omitted. In the drama, Phineas again plays the role of the white knight. In a dialogue between him and George that was added by Aiken himself. Phineas tells George about Eliza and conducts him safely to her. The family is reunited in Phineas' chamber. Eliza tells George about her escape, a dialogue that is not part of the novel, and the two of them plan their further escape with Phineas who accompanies them. What is left out by Aiken is Eliza's stay at the house of Mr. and Mrs. Bird as well as the involvement of many other Quakers – these characters don't appear in the drama at all. The second dialogue between George and Phineas is quite different compared with that of the novel. At the beginning Eliza says what is said by the Quaker Simeon Halliday in the novel. At the end it's Phineas who says what Halliday says. Some things are mixed up. What's identical is that George says that he'll fight to the last breath to defend his family, if necessary with weapons. He doesn't want anyone to get involved for him, but Phineas wants to help them by being their driver. In the last scene of the drama in which Eliza and George appear they are pursued by the slavecatchers Loker and Marks. Standing on a rock George exclaims, "I am George Harris. A Mr. Harris, of Kentucky, did call me his property. But now I'm a freeman, standing on heaven's free soil; and my wife and my child I claim as mine … I know very well that you've got the law on your side, and the power; but you haven't got us … we'll fight for our liberty till we die!" This speech is the same compared with that of the novel except for some omissions and less remarkable variations. After having said that Marks fires at George, but he's not wounded. When Loker ascends the rock, Phineas throws him over it. Marks runs away. George and Eliza are safe. This is the end of the second act of the drama and the last scene in which George and Eliza appear. From the third act on Uncle Tom is foregrounded. Stowe let them appear more often in her novel. Having shaken off their pursuers, they make their way to Canada with the help of some more activists of the "underground railroad." George finds his faith again. In Canada, they are reunited with their whole family.

Together they go to France where George studies. In a letter to a friend he tells about his plans for the future. He wants to go to Liberia with his family and be a teacher of Christianity. For Eliza and George the novel as a very happy ending. Aiken left out all those coincidences towards the end of the story, just like the emigration to Liberia. Perhaps the latter just didn´t correspond to his political ideas, and the reunion of the family was too odd and unbelievable to him. Furthermore, these passages seem to be too drywitted for a play whose main aim is to entertain an audience. That he didn´t make George a believer matches the observations of the whole drama: religious aspects didn´t play such a central role for him.

Phineas Fletcher

In opposition to the novel, the character of the Quaker Phineas Fletcher plays a considerably more important role in the drama. In Stowe´s novel he simply functions as a driver for George and Eliza on their way from the Quaker settlement to Canada. When they´re followed by Marks and Loker, he throws Loker over the rocks. In Aiken´s drama he appears much earlier. He´s the one who helps Eliza in the tavern and after she´s crossed the Ohio River, and later also George, whom he safely takes to his family. He finally defends Eliza and George against the slavecatchers Marks and Loker. Phineas is the only Quaker in the drama. One learns that he had once had a plantation with several slaves, but that he freed all of them for his beloved wife, an abolitionist, who wanted him to do so. Not only did he become an abolitionist himself, but he also became a "teetotaller", i.e. that he doesn´t drink any alcohol. The word "teetotally" is used by this cheerful and buoyant character very often making him somewhat comical.

Arthur and George Shelby

In the first chapter of the novel the reader becomes witness of a conversation between the plantation owner Arthur Shelby and the slavetrader Haley. One learns that Shelby is in debt and owes money to Haley. To pay the dues and to avoid losing the whole plantation in the end, Shelby wants to sell him his best slave, namely Tom, whose virtues he praises, about whom he says that he´s "a good, steady, sensible, pious fellow", who is "worth that sum anywhere", and Harry, whom Haley demands. It hurts Shelby to sell his slaves, but he has no other choice. In the following, one is given a description of plantation life and slavery in Kentucky as well as a characterization of Arthur Shelby. A rather positive picture of slavery is sketched in the case of plantations in Kentucky, but the narrator emphasizes "the shadow of the *law*." "So long as the law considers all these human beings, with beating hearts and living affections, only as so many *things* belonging to a master, ... so long it is impossible to make anything beautiful or desirable in the best regulated administration of slavery" (Stowe (1967) 20). Shelby himself is presented as a humane and kind gentlemen by Stowe, who really cares for his slaves. The relationship between him and his slaves is described as being good. He and especially George Shelby play a minor role for Aiken. In the drama, nearly all the scenes with George Shelby are omitted. What's left is that he tries to find Uncle Tom to bring him back home, but he arrives too late at Legree's plantation. He neither has a fight with Legree, nor does he bury Tom, nor does he free all his slaves back in Kentucky. What Aiken added is that Marks helps him find Tom. Arthur Shelby even appears only in one scene: when he talks to Haley about selling his slaves. As the character of Mrs. Shelby is omitted by Aiken, the dialogues with her are omitted as well. The dialogue between Shelby and Uncle Tom that is mentioned above is left out, too. In the drama, Arthur and George Shelby simply frame everything. The scene with Arthur Shelby keeps the plot going. For his drama, Aiken didn't choose a happy ending. Therefore, all the final scenes, among others that in which George Shelby frees his slaves, are omitted. There is an unhappy ending.

Haley, Loker and Marks

The slavetrader Dan Haley and the two slavecatchers Marks and Tom Loker are presented very similarly in both the novel and the drama. They are avaricious and coldhearted. They are strong advocates of slavery as it is the tool for them getting rich. Slaves are mere things for them. These three characters aren't transformed, but Aiken changed the plot. While in the novel Tom Loker is only wounded in the pursuit of the fugitives George and Eliza, and carried to a Quaker settlement where he becomes a better man, he dies when Phineas throws him over a rock in the drama. The Quakers of the novel were except for Phineas completely left out by Aiken – they weren't important for him. Furthermore, he wanted to come up to the expectations of his audience. Therefore, he would never have had the bad guy Loker transform into a nice, human Christian. This would have been odd and the audience wouldn´t have bought that from him. As already mentioned above, Marks later on tries to blackmail Legree and kills him in a fight. Having him play this role, Aiken provided for his amusing character Gumption Cute to appear more often. In addition to that, he brought more excitement into his play. "Haley represents slavery at one of its most morally vulnerable points, and it is important that he is portrayed not as a great villain, but rather as a shrewd businessman" (Gossett 120).

7.3. Themes

If one has a look at Stowe´s novel as a whole, certain themes that recur again and again can be made out. For one thing, the female characters are depicted as influential and powerful. In comparison with the male characters, they are often presented as morally superior. "The best people, the strongest people, the people on whom the salvation of the country rests are women. The men in the book are too deeply committed to the business of slavery either to be able to see it as a moral ans social wrong or to be able to act" (Kirkham 1102). Mrs. Bird and Mrs. Shelby play an important role in the novel as they are opponents of slavery and try to exert influence on their husbands or act selfreliantly to support the slaves. In the case of slavery, they follow the moral law rather than the law of the country. Little Eva puts the moral law above everything, too. She sees the evils of slavery and wants her slaves to be free whom she acknowledges as being equal. Besides these white female characters, the black characters of Eliza and Cassy, e.g., fight for an end of slavery as well by escaping their masters. Cassy is presented as quite rebellious by even considering to kill Legree. In some passages of her book, Stowe emphasizes the positive influence of mothers, e.g. St. Clare´s mother, and makes her female readers feel for Eliza as a mother, when her child is about to be taken away from her. All these aspects, the theme of the moral superiority of women and the theme of the sanctity of motherhood that is foregrounded in the novel, make *Uncle Tom's Cabin* feminist text. *Uncle Tom's* Cabin shows without doubt an "emphasis on domesticity" (DeLombard 153). As mentioned above, Stowe was educated by her feminist sister and poured her whole life into the novel. Aiken didn´t take over these themes. In his drama, the women play a rather passive role, take a backseat, and some female characters are even omitted. It´s the men who have the power. With Eva, however, he still has one female character who follows the moral law.

Besides the female characters, it is significant that most of the black characters of the novel are depicted as morally and spiritually superior, too, especially Uncle Tom. Wurst criticizes that "by postulating the moral and spiritual superiority of the two suppressed groups, women and black people, instead of a vision of equal adulthood, Stowe marred the political impact of the book" (Wurst 2452). In the drama, this superiority is at least applicable to Uncle Tom, who also functions as a spiritual adviser for others.

As far as morality is concerned, another theme can be made out, that of breaking the laws of the country in favor of the moral law or the law of God. George Harris as well as his wife Eliza, Senator Bird, the Quakers, and Cassy – all of them violate the law, but in the end, they triumph.

Another theme that can be made out in the novel is the sanctity of the family. There are several passages in which Stowe emphasizes that the worst evil of slavery is the separation of families. Writing about this, she gets very sentimental at times and appeals to the hearts of her readers, e.g. in the scene in which Uncle Tom talks to his wife Chloe, or in the scene in which Emmeline is separated from her mother. Such scenes were to a great extend shortened or left out by Aiken. However, howsoever passive she is presented on the whole, he took over the first part of Eliza's plot having her protect her son Harry and fight for being reunited with her husband George. Nevertheless, the relationship between the slaves and details about their family life are neglected in the drama. One doesn't learn a lot about Uncle Tom's family, and Eliza and George aren't united with their other family members in the end. Aiken didn't want to get too sentimental in his drama. Furthermore, he only focused on the main characters – otherwise his drama would have boosted out.

The theme that can be found in both the novel and the drama, the theme that recurs again and again is that of Christianity. Without doubt, religious aspects play a central role in the novel. Stowe was a very religious person herself and suggested her ideas in *Uncle Tom's Cabin*. Her novel "emphasized the role of Christian belief in liberating slaves ..." (Tushnet 103). With the characters of Uncle Tom, Eliza, and Eva there are three faithful Christians who are foregrounded. Especially Tom shows the religious traits which Stowe admired. It is his faith in God, his prayers that make him strong till the end. "Even on the godforsaken Legree plantation, Tom's presence as a religious leader is so powerful that he is able to transform even the hardened souls of the brutalized slaves" (Shackelford 1231). In the drama, religion plays an important role as well, Tom remains the faithful slave who prays for himself and his fellows, but it doesn't play such a central role compared with Stowe's novel, and, furthermore, Christianity is questioned. It is significant that in the drama neither the overseers Sambo and Quimbo, nor George Harris become Christians. Aiken presented religion as the one thing slaves could stick to in every situation of their life, he showed how it helped them in their misery, and let Eva embody Christian love, but the theme is still more foregrounded in the novel.

Although other themes play an important role in the novel, too, *Uncle Tom's Cabin* "maintains its position as an antislavery text" (Cohoon 133). Stowe started writing her famous novel, because she was enraged about the Fugitive Slave Act from 1850, and political aspects concerning the "peculiar institution" are discussed in the book. In her novel, Stowe presents the evils of slavery. The worst evil for her is the separation of families which is emphasized in several passages. It's important to notice that she doesn't aim her critique of slavery at certain people themselves, but at the system. By making Legree a Northerner she tried to show more clearly that she didn't intend to attack Southern plantation owners personally. "Stowe repeatedly emphasizes the North's involvement in slavery" (Cohoon 132). She didn't let the North remain guiltless. The character of Ophelia, who comes from Vermont, is depicted as racist, too. She has prejudices towards black people. Although she's an opponent of slavery and wants it to be abolished, she cannot imagine blacks living together with the white people. She'd prefer them to be given their freedom and leave the United States. Ophelia's attitude towards slavery comes close to Stowe's own attitude. Toward the end of her novel, George and Eliza, and several other black characters leave the country to immigrate to Liberia.[3] "Stowe's conclusions prove problematic because

---

3   The emigration of blacks to Africa had been the aim of the American Colonization Society that was founded in 1816. By 1821, the ACS had purchased a colony for the settlement of African Americans, namely Liberia (Sellman 10). "In the United States, whites advocated black emigration not to remove indigents but to banish potential insurgents" (Ammons 230).

her story does not make a place for freed slaves to live in the United States …" (Cohoon 132). For this idea, as mentioned above, she was harshly criticized by abolitionists. Aiken´s drama shares an antislavery message as well. Legree remained a Northerner, Ophelia kept her prejudices towards black people. It´s again not the Southerners who are primarily attacked personally, but the system itself. Aiken, however, didn´t go so far as to suggest what should be done after slavery has been abolished. The final chapters of the novel in which the idea of colonization is presented, weren´t taken over by Aiken. What´s emphasized both in the novel and in the drama as far as abolitionism is concerned, is the help of activists for the "underground railroad." This network was "the most important example of abolitionist direct action" (Sellman 13).

The religious and political aspects of *Uncle Tom´s Cabin* can be combined. The theme then is the clash of Christian love with its positive impacts and the institution of slavery with its evils. Uncle Tom and little Eva, who embodies Christian love, both die in the novel, but through their death they are redeemed and in the end prevail over slavery. In his drama, Aiken took over Eva´s death and, therefore, the death of "a perfect child." (Wurst 2450). The death of Uncle Tom was taken over as well. Aiken also included the scene in which he forgives his master Legree and the overseers Sambo and Quimbo.

A minor theme can be made out if one has a look at the character of Topsy. At the beginning, Topsy is very hard to handle for everyone – she nearly drives Ophelia round the bend. Of herself she says, "I ´spects I´s de wickedest critter in de world." As she explains, the reason for her being wicked is that she´s "nothing but a nigger." As a black person, Topsy thinks that she´s despised and laughed at by other people, and that no one loves her. She herself doesn´t know about loving someone for she was separated from her family very early – just like she doesn´t know about her age and other things because of that. Topsy somehow sees herself through the eyes of other people whom she tries to imitate. Her transformation begins when Eva tells her that she loves her and wants her to be better. For the first time in her life, Topsy is aware of herself being loved by someone. The theme of black people degrading themselves due to them being black was taken over by Aiken, who also let Topsy say, "I´s brack – no one loves me!"

A final theme that recurs through the whole novel is that of the contrariness or the disparity of the races. Again and again there is a clash of white and black people. Stowe, just like Aiken in his drama, made use of "racial stereotypes," for what she was often condemned as a racist (Riss 60). Certain traits are assigned to both black and white characters. Uncle Tom is presented as affectionate and submissive, forgiving and pious. Stowe found obvious virtues in the black race. In her opinion, black people "have warmth, kindliness, attachment to family, patience, meekness; they have richly emotional natures which make them susceptible to art, music, and religion" (Gossett 66). "For Stowe, the most significant personal characteristic of Africans is their essential affinity for Christianity. Negroes, as Tom most clearly demonstrates, have ´a natural genius for religion`" (Riss 63). With his white masters St. Clare and Legree, Tom has to face two agnostics. In opposition to the African characters, many white AngloSaxon characters, among others Legree, are assigned the traits of being "logical and cold" (Riss 69). Besides Tom, Topsy is another good example for a stereotyped black character, at least before her transformation. She is introduced to the reader as being "one of the blackest of her race" (Stowe (1967) 224) Topsy steals and lies, sings and dances, and is often very silly. In the scene in which Eva and Topsy talk to each other about Topsy having stolen something, the contrariness between them is best shown. As Stowe writes,

> There stood the two children, representatives of the two extremes of society. The fair, highbred child, with her golden head, her deep eyes, ... and princelike movements; and her black, keen, subtle, cringing, ... neighbor. They stood the representatives of of their races. The Saxon, born of ages of cultivation, command, education, physical and moral eminence; the Afric, born of ages of oppression, submission, ignorance, toil, and vice! (232)

The clash of the two races is also emphasized in Aiken´s play.

8. Conclusion

When Stowe's *Uncle Tom's Cabin* was published in 1851/52, it didn't take long until the story was dramatized and brought to the stage. The most popular adaptation, the one that came closest to the novel, was the one by George Aiken. Just like the novel, the play was a great success. People got into a real "Uncle Tom mania."

Although Aiken took over most of the main plot and characters of the novel for his drama, he didn't simply copy everything. Instead, he carefully selected what he included and how he did so. There were some things he changed or even excluded, and others, he added all by himself. Some of the characters of the novel don't play any role in the drama, e.g. the characters of Mrs. Shelby and Mrs. Bird. On the whole, the female characters were depicted as rather passive compared with the novel. The feminist features of the original story, the praise of motherhood and the family, as well as the description of the moral superiority of women was omitted by Aiken. Therefore, characters like Cassy and even Eliza took a backseat. Except for the passivation of some of the female characters, others were treated comically. Ophelia was reduced to her complaint about the shiftlessness of blacks. Topsy's character was extremely exaggerated and she was given comic performances and dialogues. To achieve that, Aiken added a completely new plot line to the original story and included the characters of Gumption Cute and Deacon Perry. Eva became a "sugary little simpleton," but nevertheless, she remained influential towards the male characters.

That Aiken changed all these things has a certain reason. He had another audience in mind, to whose expectations he wanted to come up to. His main aim was to entertain the people. Therefore, he also excluded most of the sentimental scenes of the novel that can be found in the context of the themes of Christianity and the sanctity of the family. Religious aspects play an important role in his drama as well, but they aren't that emphasized. The relationship between the slaves, the family ties are to a large extent neglected. What Aiken excluded as well, were all the coincidences toward the end of the story. George and Eliza aren't reunited with the rest of their family, and the idea of colonization of blacks isn't included, either.

Disregarding the differences, what both the novel and the drama share, is an antislavery message. For the political attitudes and ideas expressed in her masterpiece, Stowe not only won praise, but also received criticism. Especially the South criticized her depiction of slave owners. The people from the Southern states didn't see that Stowe didn't mean to attack people personally, but rather the institution of slavery. To emphasize that, she made Legree, by far the worst character of the story, a Northerner. Just like Stowe, Aiken didn't leave the North guiltless as far as slavery is concerned. In his drama, Legree and Ophelia are Northerners, too.

No matter whether in print or on stage, *Uncle Tom's Cabin* like no other work of that time exerted influence on the people, stirred the opponents and the advocates of slavery up against one another, made them reflect upon the "peculiar institution" more closely. Not without any reason was it said to be jointly responsible for "that great war."

9. Bibliography

Adams, John R.. *Harriet Beecher Stowe*. Boston, Massachusetts: Twayne Publishers, 1963.

Aiken, George L.. "Uncle Tom's Cabin; or, Life Among the Lowly". In: Jeffrey H. Richards, ed. *Early American Drama*. New York: Penguin Books, 1997. 373443.

"Aiken's Uncle Tom". *Uncle Tom's Cabin & American Culture*. 2009. Stephen Railton & the University of Virginia. 28 July 2009. <http://utc.iath.virginia.edu/ onstage/scripts/aikenhp.html>

Ammons, Elizabeth. *Critical Essays on Harriet Beecher Stowe*. Boston, Massachusetts: G.K. Hall & Co., 1980. xixviii.

Ammons, Elizabeth. "Freeing the Slaves and Banishing the blacks: Racism, Empire, and Africa in *Uncle Tom's Cabin*". In: Elizabeth Ammons, ed. *Harriet Beecher Stowe's Uncle Tom's Cabin: A Casebook*. New York: Oxford University Press, 2007. 22744.

Ammons, Elizabeth. *Harriet Beecher Stowe's Uncle Tom's Cabin: A Casebook*. New York: Oxford University Press, 2007. 314.

Anthony, Katharine. "Stowe, Harriet Elizabeth Beecher". In: Dumas Malone, ed. *Dictionary of American Biography*. Vol.18. London, England: Milford et al., 1936. 11520.

Bordman, Gerald. "Uncle Tom's Cabin". In: Gerald Bordman, ed. *The Oxford Companion to American Theatre*. 2nd ed.. New York: Oxford University Press, 1992. 685.

Bryer, Jackson R. "AfricanAmerican Drama". In: Jackson R. Bryer & Mary J. Hartig, eds. The Facts on File *Companion to American Drama*. New York: Facts on File, 2004. 612.

Cohoon, Lorinda B.. "Harriet Beecher Stowe". In: Jay Parini, ed. *The Oxford Encyclopedia of American Literature*. Vol.4. Oxford, England: Oxford University Press, 2004. 13035.

DeLombard, Jeannine Marie. *Slavery on Trial – Law, Abolitionism, and Print Culture*. Chapel Hill, North Carolina: University of North Carolina Press, 2007. 15156.

Ellis, Robert P. "Harriet Beecher Stowe". In: Carl E. Rollyson, ed. *Notable American Novelists*. rev. ed.. Vol.3. Pasadena, California: Salem Press, 2008. 124656.

Filler, Louis. "Antislavery Movements in the United States". In: Bernard Johnston et al., ed. *Collier's Encyclopedia: With Bibliography and Index*. New York: Collier's, 1995. 32531.

Gardner, Dr. Eric. *Major Voices: The Drama of Slavery*. New Milford, Connecticut: The Toby Press, 2005. 16569.

Gossett, Thomas F.. *Uncle Tom's Cabin and American Culture*. Dallas, Texas: Southern Methodist University Press, 1985.

Hedrick, Joan D.. "Stowe, Harriet Beecher". In: John A. Garraty & Mark C. Carnes, eds. *American National Biography*. Vol.20. New York: Oxford University Press, 1999. 90608.

Herget, Winfried. "Villains for Pleasure? The Paradox of NineteenthCentury (American) Melodrama". In: Frank Kelleter & Barbara Krah, eds. *Melodrama! The Mode of Excess from Early America to Hollywood*. Heidelberg, Germany: Winter, 2007. 1931.

Hill, Errol G. & Hatch, James V.. *A History of African American Theatre*. Cambridge, England: Cambridge University Press, 2003. ch.2.

Holmes, George F.. "Review of *Uncle Tom's Cabin*". In: Elizabeth Ammons. *Critical Essays on Harriet Beecher Stowe*. Boston, Massachusetts: G.K. Hall & Co., 1980. 724.

JordanLake, Joy. *Whitewashing Uncle Tom's Cabin: NineteenthCentury Women Novelists Respond to Stowe*. Nashville, Tennessee: Vanderbilt University Press, 2005.

Kirkham, E. Bruce. "Stowe, Harriet (Elizabeth) Beecher". In: Steven R. Serafin, ed. *Encyclopedia of American literature*. New York: Continuum, 2003. 110104.

Meserve, Walter J. *An Outline History of American Drama*. Totowa, New Jersey: Littlefield, Adams & Co., 1965.

Nathans, Heather. "Aiken, George L.". In: Jackson R. Bryer & Mary C. Hartig, ed. *The Facts On File Companion to American Drama*. New York: Facts On File, 2004. 1415.

Miller, Jordan Y.. *American Dramatic Literature: Ten Modern Plays in Historical Perspective*. New York: McGrawHill, 1961.

Richards, Jeffrey H.. *Early American Drama*. New York: Penguin Books, 1997.

Riss, Arthur. *Race, Slavery, and Liberalism in NineteenthCentury American Literature*. Cambridge: Cambridge University Press, 2006. ch.23.

Sand, George. "Review of *Uncle Tom's Cabin*". In: Elizabeth Ammons. *Critical Essays on Harriet Beecher Stowe*. Boston, Massachusetts: G.K. Hall & Co., 1980. 36.

Sellman, James. "Abolitionism in the United States". In: Kwame Anthony Appiah & Henry Louis Gates, Jr., eds. *Africana: The Encyclopedia of the African and African American Experience*. 2nd ed.. Vol.1. Oxford, England: Oxford University Press, 2005. 815.

Shackelford, Lynne. "Harriet Beecher Stowe: Uncle Tom's Cabin; or, Life Among the Lowly". In: Matthew J. Bruccoli & Judith Baughman, ed. *Student's Encyclopedia of American Literary Characters*. Vol.4. New York: Facts On File, 2008. 122532.

Stowe, Harriet Beecher. "Letter to Mrs. Follen". In: Elizabeth Ammons, ed. *Harriet Beecher Stowe's Uncle Tom's Cabin: A Casebook*. New York: Oxford University Press, 2007.

Stowe, Harriet Beecher. *Uncle Tom's Cabin*. Airmont Publishing Company, ed.. New York: Airmont Books, 1967.

Toll, Robert C.. *Blacking Up: The Minstrel Show in NineteenthCentury America*. New York: Oxford University Press, 1974.

Tushnet, Mark V.. *Slave Law in the American South: State vs. Mann in History and Literature*. Lawrence, Kansas: University Press of Kansas, 2003. 611, 97103.

Wagenknecht, Edward. *Harriet Beecher Stowe: The Known and the Unknown*. New York: Oxford University Press, 1965.

Wurst, Karin A.. "Harriet Beecher Stowe". In: Steven G. Kellman, ed. *Magill's Survey of American Literature*. rev. ed.. Vol.6. Pasadena, California: Salem Press, 2006. 244953.